FINDING FREEDOM IN CHRIST

SHARON TESCHNER

WESTBOW
PRESS®
A DIVISION OF THOMAS NELSON
& ZONDERVAN

Copyright © 2016 Sharon Teschner.

All rights reserved. No part of this book may be used or reproduced by any means, graphic, electronic, or mechanical, including photocopying, recording, taping or by any information storage retrieval system without the written permission of the author except in the case of brief quotations embodied in critical articles and reviews.

This book is a work of non-fiction. Unless otherwise noted, the author and the publisher make no explicit guarantees as to the accuracy of the information contained in this book and in some cases, names of people and places have been altered to protect their privacy.

Scripture taken from the HOLY BIBLE, NEW INTERNATIONAL VERSION. Copyright 1973, 1978, 1984, by International Bible society. Used by permission of Zondervan Publishing House. All rights reserved.

Scripture taken from New American Standard Bible copyright 1960, 1962, 1963, 1968, 1971, 1972, 1973, 1975, 1977, 1994 by the Lockman Foundation. Used by permission.

WestBow Press books may be ordered through booksellers or by contacting:

WestBow Press
A Division of Thomas Nelson & Zondervan
1663 Liberty Drive
Bloomington, IN 47403
www.westbowpress.com
1 (866) 928-1240

Because of the dynamic nature of the Internet, any web addresses or links contained in this book may have changed since publication and may no longer be valid. The views expressed in this work are solely those of the author and do not necessarily reflect the views of the publisher, and the publisher hereby disclaims any responsibility for them.

Any people depicted in stock imagery provided by Thinkstock are models, and such images are being used for illustrative purposes only. Certain stock imagery © Thinkstock.

ISBN: 978-1-5127-4891-8 (sc)
ISBN: 978-1-5127-4892-5 (e)

Library of Congress Control Number: 2016911190

Print information available on the last page.

WestBow Press rev. date: 7/28/2016

Contents

How to Use This Study Guide vii

Chapter 1   Freedom in Christ... 1

Chapter 2   Abiding in Christ 9

Chapter 3   Know Who You Are 17

Chapter 4   I Have Been Forgiven 27

Chapter 5   Managing Emotions God's Way...............................35

Chapter 6   Your Conscience: Can You Trust It?....................... 44

Chapter 7   Failure: Is It a Roadblock or Pathway to Freedom?....51

Leader's Guide..61

How to Use This Study Guide

This study can be used by for individual or group study. The goal is to learn all you can from the passage being studied. Once you know what the Bible says, make a personal application to your life.

To get the most from this section, be sure to journal your thoughts and feelings as well as any action you want to take. At the end of each chapter is space for you to make these journal notes. Journaling has many benefits.

- It increases your focus.
- It gives you a deeper level of learning.
- It boosts your memory.
- It helps give you mental clarity and to connect with your emotions.
- It helps you track what you have learned through the study.

Suggestions for Group Study

To maximize your benefit of a group study, read and study the Bible passages beforehand, come prepared to participate. As you go through the study guide questions, get everyone to participate.

If a question comes up that is not answered in the leader's guide, have several people research it, and bring the answer back next week. Be sure all answers are backed up with scripture, not what an individual thinks or feels.

Each chapter covers a subject. I recommend taking more than one session per chapter. Remember: the goal of Bible study is spiritual growth and personal application.

Start and end in prayer. Remember: the Holy Spirit is the teacher.

CHAPTER 1

Freedom in Christ

Then you will know the truth and the truth will set you free.
—John 8:32 (NIV)

The Truth Will Set You Free

Jesus said, "I have come that you might have life, and have it more abundantly." Are you enjoying your Christian life? Are you in bondage? If you feel like there must be something more, you need to know the truth; the truth is what will set you free. In John 14:6, Jesus says, "I am the truth." To know the truth is to know Jesus. Knowing who Jesus is and other facts about Him is not enough; you need to know Him as you would a close friend. Think about the words you might choose to describe a close friend. Now, think about the words you would use to describe an acquaintance. Which are the words you use to describe your relationship with Jesus?

First, Consider What Freedom Is Not

- It is not being able to do whatever you want.
- It is not without accountability to others.
- It is not without consequences for your behavior.

Now, Consider What Freedom Is

- It is being able to enjoy what Christ has given you.
- It is being free from the bondage of sin.
- It is being free from the power of your sinful nature.

To Know the Truth

Jesus told His disciples in John 8:32 that you can know the truth, and the truth will set you free. If you know Jesus, He will set you free. Are you experiencing freedom in Christ? I want to introduce you to a woman who met Jesus and found freedom.

Before continuing with this Bible study, you need to read this woman's story. You can find it in John 4:3-42.

The Bible tells the story of a woman you would think could never experience freedom. Jesus encountered her at a well outside her hometown of Sychar. Jesus and His disciples were tired and hungry from their long journey from Judea, and the disciples left Jesus at Jacob's well to go get food. Jesus saw a Samaritan woman coming to Jacob's well. When the Samaritan woman got to the well and drew water, Jesus asked her to draw a drink of water for Him. Now, the Samaritan woman instantly knew that he was a Jew by the way he dressed. A Jewish man from Judea would have had no dealings with any Samaritans—especially a Samaritan woman. To ask for a drink from her cup would make a Jew ceremonially unclean. It would mean that he would not be able to worship at the temple until he had gone through the process of becoming ceremonially clean. When the Samaritan women questioned Jesus, He replied, "If you knew the gift of God and who it is that asks you for a drink, you would have asked Him, and He would have given you living water."

1. Why do you think Jesus asked this woman for a drink?

   Asking for the drink was a way for Jesus to begin a conversation. Jesus immediately turned the conversation from His need to her need. His need was obviously that of physical thirst and a need for a drink of water. Jesus knew that the woman had a greater need than His. He wanted to talk with her about how she could know God personally.

   Jesus stated that He would have given her the gift of God and living water if she would have asked. She did not understand what Jesus meant by "the gift of God" and "living water." The gift of God that Jesus was offering to her was salvation. Salvation is a gift to those who ask. Water is what gives us physical life, and living water is what gives us spiritual life. Once the woman showed interest in what Jesus offered her, Jesus asked her to go and get her husband.

2. How did she respond to His request to call her husband (John 4:17)?

3. After the woman told Jesus she had no husband, what did Jesus tell her (John 4:18)?

   Jesus agreed with her, explaining that she had been married five times and was currently living with a man to whom she was not married. Jesus asked her to go get her husband to reveal her sin and give her an opportunity to confess. By verbally admitting her sin, she took a necessary step toward finding the freedom that Jesus offers to all who come to Him. When Jesus revealed to her that she has had five husbands and that the man she now lives with is not her husband, she called Jesus a prophet and asked Him yet another question.

4. What did she ask Jesus (John 4:20)?

5. What do you think is the importance of this question to the woman?

The Jews worshipped at the temple in Jerusalem. They believed the only place God dwelled was in the Holy of Holies. Therefore, the only place they could worship the one true God was in the Jerusalem temple. The Samaritans worshipped God in a temple on Mount Gerizim. The Samaritans had long been separated from the Jews for both religious and political reasons. After a discussion on worship, the Samaritan woman believed that Jesus is the promised Messiah.

6. What did the Samaritan woman believe (John 4:21–29)?

7. After she believed, what was the woman's response (John 4:28–29)?

After the Samaritan woman believed Jesus to be the promised Messiah, she did something that was very important. She left her water pot and went to share what she had learned with other people. There may be things in your life you must leave behind in order to move forward with your new life in Christ. It is through this process of leaving things behind and sharing your experiences that you find a greater freedom in your spiritual life. You find your spiritual needs are more important than your physical needs.

The disciples brought food back with them and wanted Jesus to eat. Jesus stated that He had food that they did not know about, thus perplexing the disciples. As Jesus often did, He used a physical illustration to teach a spiritual truth. Jesus used the concept of our bodies needing food to teach the disciples how important His work on earth was. Jesus came to restore the broken relationship between God and humankind.

8. In John 4:32–38, Jesus explained the spiritual truth He wanted the disciples to learn. What was Jesus teaching His disciples?

Earlier in the story, it stated that Jesus had to pass through Samaria. After meeting the Samaritan woman and the people from Sychar, Jesus stayed a couple of days. We can learn much from Jesus's behavior. Jesus's plans changed when He found people who were interested in spiritual things. It did not matter to Jesus who the people were. He was always willing to share God's plan of salvation with anyone. Jesus was willing to alter His plans to meet the spiritual needs of people.

Make It Personal

There are many excuses Jesus could have given for not talking to the Samaritan woman—He was tired, He needed to eat, or His feet were hurting from traveling. His physical needs were not unlike our needs, yet He made the spiritual needs of others His priority. Is there someone in your life with whom you should be sharing Christ?

Points to Ponder

When you consider the Samaritan woman and who she was, you understand the barriers in this woman's life that were preventing her from experiencing freedom in Christ.

- She was a Samaritan, the lowest socioeconomic group of people. The Samaritans were considered to be half-breeds, and they were despised by the Jews. Samaritans were so despised by the Jews that they would not travel through Samaria. Instead, they would walk miles around to get where they were going.
- She had been married five times and was currently living with a man without being married. This made her an outcast in society. One indication of this is the fact that she was drawing water at noon, in the heat of the day, instead of early morning with the rest of the women from the city.
- Jesus shows us through His encounter with the Samaritan woman that no one is beyond finding freedom in Christ. John 8:31–32 says, "The truth will make you free." Jesus says in John 14:6, "I am the way and the truth and the life," making it clear that if we want to be free we must know Jesus.

Dig Deeper

Share with each other what you think it means to know Jesus.

Is Jesus the Lord or ruler of your life? If you are to make Jesus the Lord of your life, what changes might you consider making?

Now, share those changes with the group. You might say, "Wait a minute. I don't want to share stuff like that. It's too personal!" In James 5:16, we see a direct command by God to share those things we want to keep to ourselves. God tells us to share the secret things of our heart because He knows that in sharing them, they lose the strong hold they have on us. We must let others help us on life's journey to find freedom.

Prayer Requests

♥ **Make It Personal: Journal Notes** ♥

CHAPTER 2

Abiding in Christ

So Jesus was saying to those who believed in Him, "If you abide in my word, then you are truly disciples of mine. And you will know the truth and the truth will set you free."
—John 8:31–32 (NAS)

Jesus has told you how you can be His disciple. If it is your desire to be set free, there are things that you must learn and things that you must do to find the freedom Jesus has told you about. You must know the truth to be set free. Jesus has promised you freedom, but it requires something from you. At the completion of this chapter, you will be able to answer the following questions from God's point of view.

- What does it mean "to abide in my word"?
- What does it mean to truly be a disciple of Jesus?
- What does it mean for you to know the truth?
- What is the truth setting you free from?

Take some time to discuss the following questions with the group. Before proceeding with this lesson make some journal notes. By keeping this journal, you will be able to see yourself grow spiritually.

- If I asked you what it means to abide, what would you tell me?
- What do you think these verses say about being set free?

If You Abide in My Word

"If you abide in my word," are the words Jesus starts with in John 8:31. The word "if" is a conjunction, a conditional clause; it assumes an action will be done. It puts a condition on the statement that follows it and requires the action to be done to get the final results. Here the assumed action is that you will abide in the way Jesus has been teaching. To better understand what the phase, "if you abide in my word," means, I recommend reading John 8:31–32 in various translations. You will see the words, "if you abide in me," stated in different ways, such as, "if you hold to my teaching," or, "if you continue in my word."

Also, if you consider some synonyms for the word "abide," it will give you a better understanding of what "to abide" means. Some synonyms are: to obey, to observe, to act in accordance with, to dwell with or reside with.

To me, this passage means I am continually saturated by the Word of God and choose to do the things that please God.

The words of Jesus, "if you abide in my word," are a prerequisite to all that follows. You need to find ways to be fully saturated with the teachings of Jesus so that you can be His disciple. As Jesus's disciple, you will know the truth and find the freedom God promises.

Ways to Abide in My Word

The following verses will give some ways you can abide in Christ. Match the following verses with ways you can abide.

a. Acts 24:14   ___defend your faith
b. Psalm 119:11   ___believe everything written in the law and prophet
c. Joshua 1:8   ___think on things that pleasing God
d. 2 Timothy 2:15   ___go and make other disciples
e. Luke 11:28   ___memorize scripture
f. Philippians 1:16   ___when you hear what God says in His Word you do it
g. Philippians 4:8   ___meditate on scripture day and night
h. Matthew 28:19–20   ___accurately study and share the Word of God

Be Creative

Can you come up with other ways you can abide in Christ?

Personal Application

Spiritual growth is all about how you apply what you know. Consider these eight ways of abiding. Rate yourself on a scale of 1–10 (1 = needs improvement, 10 = needs no improvement).

I believe everything written in the law and prophets.	1 2 3 4 5 6 7 8 9 10
I memorize scripture.	1 2 3 4 5 6 7 8 9 10
I meditate on scripture day and night.	1 2 3 4 5 6 7 8 9 10
I study the Word of God.	1 2 3 4 5 6 7 8 9 10
When I hear what God says in His Word, I do it.	1 2 3 4 5 6 7 8 9 10
I defend my faith.	1 2 3 4 5 6 7 8 9 10

I think on things that are pleasing to God.   1 2 3 4 5 6 7 8 9 10
I share the gospel.   1 2 3 4 5 6 7 8 9 10

Share with the group your strongest area and your weakest area. Choose one area you are willing to make a commitment to improve on this week. In the journal notes, write down the area you have chosen to improve. Then write how you plan to accomplish these improvements.

A True Disciple

The NIV Bible states John 8:31 this way: "To the Jews who believed in Him," Jesus said. "If you hold to my teaching, you are really my disciples." I cannot find a clearer way to express that a disciple of Jesus is a person who does what Jesus teaches.

1. What does Luke 6:40 tell us a true disciple will be like?

> A true disciple will be just like his teacher; we should be like Jesus. As a disciple of Jesus, your life should always be in the process of becoming more like Jesus. Luke 6:40 speaks of a disciple being fully trained; you are in that process. When an athlete is in training, he or she focuses on the goal and does not let things be a distraction. In your life you have many things that distract you from your goal of being like Jesus. You may not consider these things to be sin, but they do keep you from growing spiritually. Therefore, to grow spiritually, you choose not to do these things.

Personal Growth

Discuss the following questions with your Bible study group, and take time to write in your journal notes at the end of the chapter.

- How does your life compare to the life of Christ?
- Is your focus on becoming more like Christ?
- What things are distracting you?

Jesus laid aside His Godhead. He chose to be born a man and to die a brutal, humiliating death for you. His sacrifice should cause you to ask if there are things you can lay aside for Jesus. Be sure to make a note in your journal of the things you can lay aside for Jesus.

You Will Know the Truth

In John 8:32, Jesus tells you that you will know the truth. In order to know the truth, you must be continuing in His teaching. Jesus explains why some people struggle and do not know the truth. Read John 8:43-47 and answer the following questions.

2. Why does Jesus say some people do not hear or understand?

3. In Matthew 7:13-14, what does Jesus teach about finding the way?

The Truth Sets You Free

Some people think if you are set free your life will become free of all problems. You can do whatever you want. These ideas are misconceptions of what freedom in Christ is. As you know the truth, you come to understand what freedom in Christ is. You have the freedom to become what God created you to be. In Romans 12:2, it states that your mind must be renewed. You must throw out your old way of thinking and replace it with what Jesus teaches.

4. According to John 8:34, what are you free from?

5. You are free from sin. You are free from the hold sin has on you. Yes, you have power over sin. The following verses explain you are no longer in bondage to sin but can find freedom in Christ. You have the freedom to say no to the flesh and no to the devil. You do not have to do the sinful things the flesh wants you to do. What do the following verses say about bondage?

   - Romans 6:6–7

   - Romans 6:14

Finding the Freedom in Christ You Seek

Freedom comes as you have the ability to say no to sin. This ability comes from God. It starts with a personal relationship with God and continues as you live a life in obedience to God. You are replacing the old life with a new life in Christ. As you are obedient to Christ, you experience the freedom to become what God wants you to be. You are free to love, worship, and serve God.

Make It Personal

Discuss these questions with your Bible study group. Make journal notes. Are you experiencing freedom in Christ? What is it that keeps you from experiencing the freedom God says you can have in John 8:31–32?

Dig Deeper

6. What do the following scriptures tell you about abiding in Christ?

    - 1 John 3:24

    - 1 John 3:6

    - 1 John 2:27

    - 1 John 4:13

Prayer Requests

 **Make It Personal: Journal Notes**

CHAPTER 3

Know Who You Are

We are God's workmanship created in
Christ Jesus to do good works.
—Ephesians 2:10 (NAS)

When you close your eyes and think about yourself, who is the person you see? This is your self-image. Do you like yourself? Do you hate yourself? As a disciple of Jesus, why does it matter what you think about yourself? The way you see yourself will determine how you act. When you struggle with your self-image, you are unable to reach your full potential. As a disciple of Jesus Christ, you must learn to see yourself as God sees you. Only when you have the right attitude about yourself are you able to be fully used by God. People are often full of pride and think more of themselves than they should, or they think too little of themselves. Both attitudes will keep God from being able to use you to your full potential.

The Way You Think Is How You Act

Is it possible God wants to bless you, but you won't let Him? Yes, that's right; you won't let Him. Is your attitude about yourself getting in the way of God blessing you? In Numbers chapters 13 and 14, you can see how the nation of Israel viewed themselves and how their faulty thinking kept them from entering Canaan. Moses had led the nation of Israel from Egypt to the land of Canaan, the land God had promised them. When they reached Canaan, God told Moses to send twelve men to explore the land. After spending forty days in Canaan, they were to bring back a report.

1. What is the report these men gave to Moses and to all the people (Numbers 13:26–28)?

2. What was Caleb's response (Numbers 13:30)?

3. What is the response of the other men who explored the land (Numbers 13:32–33)?

The men compared themselves to grasshoppers and the men of Canaan to giants. These men failed to see themselves as God saw them. When you think poorly of yourself and do not see yourself the way God sees you, I call this grasshopper thinking. When you have grasshopper thinking, it can have devastating consequences in your life. The trip from Egypt to Canaan should have taken about two weeks. Yet the nation of Israel wandered in the wilderness for forty years. This, I believe, was the consequence of their complaining and their grasshopper thinking.

When you see a difficult situation, do you have grasshopper thinking? Do you see how hard the situation is and feel like you are inadequate? Find a verse in the Bible that would encourage you at these difficult times. Write it in the journal notes, and memorize it.

4. The Israelites responded emotionally to the bad report the men gave. Describe the response of the Israelites (Numbers 14:1–4).

You and I are often like the Israelites. We respond emotionally. We make poor decisions or let others make the decision for us. Then we cry and complain about our lives just as the Israelites did. The Israelites blamed Moses and Aaron and accepted no responsibility for their own choices. We often fail to listen to God's instructions and then cry and blame God for our situations.

5. Two of the spies, Caleb and Joshua, spoke out to the Israelites. They shared what they believe is God's plan for the Israelites. What did Caleb and Joshua believe God would do for the Israelites (Numbers 14:8–9)?

Joshua and Caleb told the Israelites that God would give them the land. God had removed His protection from Canaan and was with the Israelites. God wanted to bless His people. God is waiting to bless you. Does your poor attitude about yourself keep you from obtaining the blessings God has for you? When you abide in Christ, you will have a healthy view of yourself. You then experience freedom in Christ, and God can use you to your full potential. You will experience blessings in your life that are unbelievable. You must be willing, like Caleb and Joshua, to trust God in situations that look hopeless.

Do You Have a Healthy Self-Image?

Compare a healthy self-image to a poor self-image. Circle the words that best describe you.

accepts self: weakness and strengths	does not trust self
open with others	always wears a mask
shows confidence	questions own ability
willing to share with others	hides from others, self, and God
will do one's best	cannot accept failure
can relate with other people	believes everything people say

See Yourself through God's Eyes

Your feelings of self-worth and acceptance must come from God. As a believer in Jesus Christ, you are told in 2 Corinthians 5:17 that you are a new creature; the old has passed away. God provides everything you need to have a healthy self-image. God provides you a sense of belonging, a sense of value, and sense of competency. Write next to each verse what it says about your belonging, your worthiness, or your competency.

- Psalm 139:14–16

- Genesis 1:26–27

- John 15:9

- Hebrews 12:6–7
- 2 Corinthians 12:9
- Matthew 6:26
- John 17:22–23
- Philippians 4:13

There Are Many Enemies to a Healthy Self-Image

As disciples of Jesus Christ, Satan will do anything he can to make you noneffective for God. Keeping you from viewing yourself as God does is one of Satan's most effective weapons. Satan wants to keep you from reaching your full potential in serving God. Consider a few of the enemies to a healthy Christian self-image.

The Enemy of Sin and Guilt

From the very beginning you can see how sin, guilt, and shame are destructive to your self-image. In the book of Genesis, Adam and Eve walked with God. When they thought they could be like God, they disobeyed Him and ate from the forbidden tree. When they disobeyed God, they sinned. Sin changed everything. The next time God came to walk with Adam and Eve, they tried to hide from Him.

6. Why do you think they tried to hide from God (Genesis 3:10)?

When Adam and Eve sinned, their self-images changed. They saw their nakedness. They now experienced feelings of fear, guilt, and shame for the very first time. They felt insecure, inferior, and inadequate. The very opposite of what you need for a healthy self-image. All the things you need for a healthy self-image are at risk when you sin. Adam and Eve then tried to fix things themselves. They tried covering their naked bodies, but it did not help. They could not fix the spiritual and emotional damage sin caused. When you sin, there is only one answer to the problem. The answer is to ask God to forgive you. When you sin you should feel guilt. As a result of this guilt, you confess your sin and accept God's forgiveness. Your broken relationship with God is then restored.

Your Spiritual Relationship

When you sin, what feelings do you experience? Are they the same emotions that Adam and Eve felt when they sinned? How do these feelings affect your personal relationship with God?

The Enemy of Comparison

When you take your eyes off of God, you often start comparing yourself with someone else. God makes it clear in His Word what He thinks of comparing yourself to someone else.

7. What does 2 Corinthians 10:12 tell you about the person who compares himself or herself to another person?

When you compare yourself to other people, you are using humankind's standards, not God's standards, to determine your worth and value. God states in Ephesians 4:18 that human understanding is darkened. It states in 2 Corinthians 3:14 that it is only in Christ that this darkened veil can be removed. God wants you to use your spiritual eyes and see yourself the way He sees you. When you compare yourselves to others, God says you are without understanding.

The Enemy of Listening to Other People

When you listen to the criticism of other people and accept it as true, you are using the wrong standard of measurement. Use a discerning ear and the Word of God to evaluate what was said.

8. In Ecclesiastes 7:21–22, the wisest king in the Bible, King Solomon, gives you a warning about listening to other people. What does King Solomon tell you in these verses?

9. In Jeremiah 29:11, what does God say about the plans He has for you?

It is often necessary for you to change how you see your future. God's plan for you is a future full of hope. When you focus on people and not God, your perceptions are always faulty. You must focus on the plans God has for you.

Your Thoughts Can Be the Enemy

What you think about will determine how you see yourself. There is a self-generated dialogue that takes place in your mind. You may have heard this referred to as self-talk. In scripture, when a person talks to himself or herself, the individual will say, "O my soul." Deborah encouraged herself with self-talk in Judges 5:21. In the book of Psalms, David frequently shares his self-talk. In Psalm 103:2, he is blessing the Lord, and in Psalm 42:5, David expresses his despair.

10. According to Proverbs 23:7, why is your self-talk important?

11. What does 2 Corinthians 10:5 tell you to do with each and every thought?

I call this taking out the trash. Thoughts that do not agree with God are trash. You and I need to take out the trash. You would not keep trash on your kitchen table, so why do you keep it in your mind? Take your wrong thinking and get rid of it! Immediately replace it with what God says. It is very important for you to replace each negative or false idea with the truth. If you do not replace the wrong thinking, it will continue to come back into your mind. Replacing the lies you believe with the truth is the only pathway to finding freedom. God says what you think is what you will become.

Make It Personal

What things do you tell yourself that God does not agree with? Now, replace them with what God says. To help you, here are a few possibilities: I must have everyone's approval; the Christian life should be easy.

Dig Deeper

Make a list of all the things you say to yourself. Place a star next to those things that agree with what God says about you. Next to the things that do not agree with what God says write what He says. Every time your self-talk does not agree with God's truth, immediately replace it with what God says is true about you.

Prayer Requests

♥ **Make It Personal: Journal Notes**

CHAPTER 4

I Have Been Forgiven

There is now no condemnation for
those who are in Christ Jesus.
—Romans 8:1 (NIV)

Accepting God's Forgiveness

I know I am a Christian. I know I am forgiven by God, but I do not feel forgiven. Instead of feeling free, I feel guilty all the time. I question why? What is wrong with me? Are these some of the feelings you struggle with? God's unconditional love and forgiveness are very difficult concepts for people to accept. In John 8:3–11, read the story of a woman Jesus loved and forgave. The Pharisees bring a woman they caught in adultery to Jesus. By quoting Old Testament law, they were hoping to trap Jesus. Without disregarding the law, Jesus finds a way He can respond to the Pharisees while showing forgiveness and unconditional love to the woman.

1. According to the law, what penalty did the scribes and Pharisees think this woman deserved (John 8:4–5)?

2. Jesus takes His time in responding. Jesus did something very odd instead of giving them an immediate answer. What does Jesus do (John 8:6)?

3. When Jesus does respond, what does he suggest to the scribes and Pharisees (John 8:7)?

4. Jesus then goes back to writing on the ground. Scripture does not tell us what he was writing, but it does give us the results. When Jesus straightens up, all of those who had accused the woman were gone. What does Jesus ask the woman (John 8:10)?

When you sin, God responds to you with this same love and forgiveness. In 1 John 1:9, it tells you that when you can confess your sins to God, you receive His forgiveness. Confessing your sin means you agree with God that what you did was wrong, and you want to turn away from your sinful behavior and turn toward Him. God is the only one who cleanses you from your sin and removes your condemnation. You need to accept His forgiveness, and stop condemning yourself.

5. Just for fun, let's speculate. What do you think Jesus could have written on the ground?

What about My Sinful Past?

6. God tells you how to deal with your past. Second Corinthians 5:17 and Philippians 3:13 describe two important approaches to responding to your past. What are these ways?

An Example of a Changed Life

The apostle Paul is the greatest example of how your life can change. His life changed so much that the name he was known by changed from Saul to Paul.

7. What activities was Saul participating in before his conversion (Acts 8:3)?

8. Acts 9:1–19 gives Saul's conversion experience. Write a brief description of Saul's conversion.

Paul had a Jewish mother and Roman father, and both a Hebrew name and a Roman one. Being a Pharisee, he used his Jewish name, Saul. After his conversion to Christ, he became known by his Roman name, Paul. I believe this was also a way for him to put his past behind him and begin a new life in Christ (Acts 16:37; 22:3, 25).

Spiritual Growth

Saul's conversion was a dramatic experience, resulting in dramatic changes to his life. What changes have occurred in your life because of your faith in Jesus Christ? Take the time to make journal notes.

But I Do Not Feel Forgiven

When you ask God to forgive you, you need to accept His forgiveness. Just as you were saved by faith, you must accept God's forgiveness by faith. You also need to forgive yourself! If God chose to forgive you, who are you to disagree with Him? Hanging on to guilt and shame keeps you in bondage. This emotional bondage keeps God from using you to your full potential. Guilt says, "I did something wrong; I made a mistake." Shame says, "I am a mistake," or, "I am worthless." Shame is different from guilt. Shame leaves you feeling hopeless. It is important to accept by faith that what God says about you is true.

9. In Romans 7:23–24, what statement does Paul make that shows he struggled with feelings of shame?

Paul, when he was known as Saul, had persecuted and killed Christians. In Acts 7:58–59, Paul had been there for the stoning of Stephen. Just like Paul, you have things in your life you wish you had never done. God forgave Paul, and He forgives you.

10. Where does Paul find freedom from the shame he feels (Romans 7:25)?

11. After Paul states what a miserable person he is, he continues writing, telling you what Christ has done for him. According to Romans 8:1–2, what does Paul tell you Christ has done for you?

Your Position in Christ

Your position in Christ means when God looks at you, a believer in Jesus Christ, He sees the pure, holy, and spotless Christ. Scripture tells you that when you accept Jesus Christ as your Savior, you become a new creation; all things have become new (2 Corinthians 5:17). By filling in the blanks below, you will discover a few of the things God has given you at salvation.

- Galatians 2:20: It is no longer I, but_____ lives in me.
- Ephesians 1:5: I am adopted into the_____.
- 2 Corinthians 5:21: I am _____.
- Romans 5:1: I am _____ (declared righteous) by God.
- Ephesians 1:1: I am a_____.
- Ephesians 1:4: I am _____.
- Ephesians 1:3: I have_____.
- Ephesians 2:6: I am seated with_____.

12. In 1 Corinthians 2:9 (NIV), it says, "No eye has seen, no ear has heard, no mind has conceived, what God has prepared for those who love Him." God has provided the Holy Spirit to show you all the things He has prepared for you. What do the following verses tell you the Holy Spirit will do for you?

    John 14:26: The Holy Spirit is our _____ and He will_____.

    John 16:13: When the Spirit comes He will _____.

1 Corinthians 2:10–16: The Spirit shows us the _____.

The Spirit is from _____. The things of the Spirit are _____ to the natural man. The Spirit gives us the _____ of Christ.

1 Corinthians 12:13–14: we are all baptized into one _____ and we all receive the _____.

With the many gifts God has given you, it would seem impossible not to feel safe and secure in His care. Yet, when shame consumes you, you do not feel safe and secure. Remember when the Israelite men saw the "giants" in the land of Canaan and they felt like grasshoppers? Your thinking can also be distorted. God has given to you a Helper. This Helper empowers you to do every task God asks of you.

As a believer, you have a new life free of condemnation. You are free from the bondage of sin. As you walk in the power of the Spirit, you are freed from guilt and shame. Growing spiritually can be slower and more difficult than you would like it to be.

Make It Personal

Change what you tell yourself. If you say things like, "I am worthless, I am a mistake, I am unacceptable," you are suffering with shame. Only by changing what you tell yourself will you begin to change how you feel. To change the way you think and what you say to yourself, you must be in God's Word. Answer the following questions.

Are you in the Word daily?

How are you renewing your mind?

Are you memorizing scripture?

Do you meditate on scripture?

How much time do you spend in prayer?

Need help? Find an accountability partner.

Dig Deeper

13. What do these verses teach you about God's forgiveness?

- 1 John 2:12

- Ephesians 1:17

- Psalm 103:12

- Colossians 1:13

- Psalm 32:5

- Hebrews 10:17

Prayer Requests

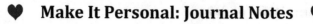 **Make It Personal: Journal Notes**

CHAPTER 5

Managing Emotions God's Way

Search me oh God and know my heart.
—Psalm 139:23 (NIV)

These things called emotions often take you on a roller-coaster ride. Can you identify the emotion you feel right now? Sometimes you feel very anxious, excited, or happy. Sometimes you feel discouraged, depressed, or down in the dumps. Often you cannot see what's coming next, and your emotions can suddenly change. How do you cope with this inner turmoil? Why did God give you emotions? Are emotions good or evil? Is following my emotions the right thing to do? The answer to all these questions is in God's Word.

Why Did God Give You Emotions?

You are created with emotions because God has emotions. God created humankind in His image and likeness so that God can have a personal relationship with us.

1. What are the emotions God expressed in the following verses?

- Numbers 32:13

- Psalm 37:13

- Judges 2:18

- Psalm 78:40

- John 3:16

- Psalm 5:5

- Exodus 20:5

James 1:17 tells you every good gift is from God. Your emotions are a good gift from God. That gift enables you to experience the rich, full, abundant life God has planned for you.

2. What emotion does God express toward us in 1 John 4:10?

3. God loved you first and sought a relationship with you. It is in His love you find the fullness of life you seek. According to 1 John 3:16–17, how do you see the love of God in action?

4. According to Philippians 4:7 and 1 Thessalonians 5:16, when you allow God's love to captivate your heart, what emotions will dominate your life?

Sin Affected Your Emotions

5. Immediately after sinning, there was an impact on Adam and Eve's emotions. What emotions did Adam and Eve experience after sinning (Genesis 3:7–8)?

To sin is to disobey God. When Adam and Eve ate from the Tree of Good and Evil, they disobeyed God. Immediately, they saw their nakedness and experienced guilt, fear, and shame. Sin took from them their innocence and their purity. Now, as a result of sin, they have a sinful nature living within. This sinful nature creates within a person the desire to please self more than the desire to please another person. As a result of this sinful nature, they saw their nakedness and experienced a sexual lust for each other. God gave us sexual desire to mutually please each other, but sin changed this mutual pleasure into a desire for self-gratification. Adam and Eve tried to cover their nakedness, but their feelings of guilt, fear, and shame were so powerful they were not able to hide from the emotions within themselves. Then Adam and Eve try to hide from God, but were unable to hide from Him.

Your Spiritual Relationship

Do the emotions of guilt, fear, and shame keep you from experiencing the abundant life God desires for you? Do you try to cover or hide from emotions that make you uncomfortable? Take time to write in the journal notes about the emotions you struggle with. Do this in the form of a prayer to God, expressing the emotions you want God's help with.

The Sin Nature

You see how sin changed the very nature of humankind. When God created people, they had a natural desire to please Him. But as a result of sin, humans wanted to please themselves. When you accept Jesus Christ as your Savior, God gives you a new nature.

6. When it comes to your sinful nature, what hope does Galatians 5:24 give those who belong to Christ?

7. To give you control over your sinful nature, what instructions does God give in Ephesians 4:22–24?

You must make a conscious choice not to satisfy the desires of the sinful nature. You must only let thoughts that are pleasing to God dwell in your mind. You choose to let the new nature have total control over your thought life. This new nature has power over the old nature. Think of it as if you have removed an old, torn, dirty shirt and are putting a clean, fresh, beautiful, new shirt. When you take off the old, you discard it and immediately replace it with the new.

Responding to Life's Circumstances

To understand and manage your emotions, you must know it is not your circumstances but your thoughts and beliefs about those circumstances that generate your emotional response. In just seconds you go through this process: an event occurs, your beliefs produce a thought, you respond to that thought with an emotion, and you then choose your actions.

You can see how an ungodly belief will cause you to act in a manner that displeases God. Therefore, two people will respond differently to the same event. It is important that your mind is completely saturated with the Word of God so that what you believe will cause your emotions and actions to give glory to God.

Damaged Emotions

If you have been emotionally hurt in your past, this can cause your emotions to stop developing and you to respond inappropriately. I call these damaged emotions. Emotional damage can come from early relationships in which love was conditional or in which you were rejected, abandoned, or hurt by an individual in your life. Experiences with harsh punishment or criticism can leave emotional scars. Theses scars remain even though the person who hurt you is no longer in your life. Your emotions need healing. This healing process begins as you choose to put on the new nature.

8. What is necessary for the healing of your damaged emotions (Romans 12:2)?

As you replace your way of thinking with what God says, your mind is renewed. Your emotions will now begin the healing process so that your emotions can function in the way God intended.

9. What promise does God give in Psalm 147:3?

God's Intentions for Your Emotions

10. Emotions were intended to be a gift from God so you could experience a full, rich, abundant life. Next to each verse, write what the Bible tells you the abundant life will look like.

    - Galatians 5:22–23

    - Colossians 3:2–3

    - 1 Corinthians 2:9

    - Ephesians 3:20

11. What does Philippians 1:21 require for you to experience the abundant life?

Emotions Are Intended to Motivate You to Take Action

12. Consider the following verses. What emotion is felt, who felt it, and what action was taken as a result of that emotion:

    - John 3:16

    - 1 Samuel 1:10

    - 1 Samuel 18:8–11

Your emotions are to motivate you to take action. What action you choose to take is entirely up to you. You cannot always control your circumstances, but you can control how you respond to them. When your mind has been renewed by spending time in God's Word, you are able to respond to your circumstances in a way that gives glory to God. You will be able to respond like Hannah and not like King Saul.

Spiritual Growth

This week pay attention to how you respond emotionally to the circumstances in your life. Write in the journal notes how you responded emotionally and if that emotional response caused you to take any actions. Also note if you thought the actions you chose pleased God.

Dig Deeper

13. Think of a time in the Old Testament when God expressed emotions. What emotion did He express, and how was it shown?

14. Think of the emotions Jesus expressed. What emotions did He express, and how did His actions express those emotions?

15. If God gave us emotions, why do you think some people view some emotions as sinful?

A Warning

In John 10:10, Jesus said He came that you might have abundant life. You have an enemy who is a thief and who comes to steal that life away from you. That thief is the devil. He wants nothing more than to make a Christian ineffective for God. One of the ways the devil can steal the abundant life from you is to get you to live by your emotions rather than by the Word of God.

16. According to 1 Peter 5:8, how does the devil operate?

17. When the enemy comes to steal the abundant life from you, what does James 4:7 tell you to do?

The devil uses your emotions to deceive you. The very first thing is that you must submit to God for it is through His power that you are able to resist the devil.

Prayer Requests

♥ Make It Personal: Journal Notes ♥

CHAPTER 6

Your Conscience: Can You Trust It?

> Keep a good conscience so that in the thing
> you are slandered, those who revile your good
> behavior in Christ will be put to shame.
> —1 Peter 3:19 (NAS)

Your Conscience

"What is your conscience?" If you ask a child this question, they might describe it as "A spot that burns inside of me when I am bad." Your conscience creates a sense of guilt that comes when you violate your inner code of conduct. Guilt can be described as a measure of disapproval of one's own self. In Romans 2:14–15, we learn all people have an innate sense of right or wrong. In other words, God has given us a conscience.

1. As a disciple of Jesus, you want your inner code of conduct to be based on what Jesus teaches, not what you think or feel. Read the following verses, and write next to each one what it tells you about your conscience.

- Acts 23:1

- Acts 24:15–16

- 1 Peter 3:16

- Hebrews 13:18

2. These verses describe a _____ or _____ conscience. As a disciple of Jesus, God's Word makes it clear that this is the type of conscience we are to maintain.

3. Titus 1:15 describes a _____ conscience. We do not start our life with a good conscience but, rather, with a conscience that has been damaged by sin. Hebrews 9:14 tells us that _____ will _____ our conscience. After salvation, the process of renewing our mind and cleansing our conscience begins.

4. In 1 Corinthians 8:7, a _____ conscience is described.

A weak conscience belongs to a spiritually immature believer. The weak conscience will produce false guilt. False guilt originates from breaking your code of conduct and from the lies the devil tells you. The devil is also called "the accuser" in Revelation 12:10. He will get you to focus on your sin rather than on God's forgiveness. A person with a weak conscience will then feel guilty for sin God has already forgiven. God asks believers who are spiritually mature and have a good, clear conscience to watch over the believer with a weak conscience. God gives us instructions on how to help those believers with a weak conscience in 1 Corinthians 8:1–13.

5. According to 1 Corinthians 8:7–12, what should a more spiritually mature believer do to help someone with a weak conscience?

Ask Yourself

What behavior could you change to help someone with a conscience weaker than your own?

Paul Teaches Timothy

6. As Paul writes a letter to Timothy, he includes instructions about the conscience. Next to each verse, write what it teaches about the conscience.

- 1 Timothy 1:5

- 1 Timothy 1:18–19

- 1 Timothy 3:8–9

- 1 Timothy 4:1–2

- 2 Timothy 1:3

From the verses you just read, answer questions 7 through 10.

7. As a believer, when you choose to ignore what is right, what happens to your conscience?

8. What are the consequences when you deliberately continue to violate your conscience?

9. Describe the different types of consciences Paul taught Timothy about.

10. Why do you think Paul took the time to teach Timothy these things about our consciences?

Match the following verses with the correct statements about your conscience.

a. 1 Timothy 1:19   ____ having a clear conscience I remember you in prayer

b. 1 Timothy 3:9   ____ I have lived before God with a clear conscience

c. 2 Timothy 1:3   ____ committed to their faith, having a clear conscience

d. Acts 23:1   ____ keep a clear conscience before man and God

e. Acts 24:16   ____ love comes from a pure heart, a genuine heart, a clear conscience

f. 1 Timothy 1:5 ___ rejecting a good conscience can ship wreck your faith

David Listens to His Conscience

When you have a clear conscience, God uses it to help you make good choices. Read the story of a man who listens to his conscience in 1 Samuel 24:1–7. Now, answer the following questions.

11. What was the action that might have been expected of David?

12. When David came close to Saul, what action did he take?

13. What effect did this action have on David's conscience?

14. How did this change David's behavior toward his men?

15. As you consider how your conscience operates, what can you learn from David's example?

Make It Personal

Can you think of a time in your life when because of your conscience you made a different choice?

Dig Deeper

16. After reading the following verses, write next to each one what it says about the Holy Spirit and about the conscience. Then answer the question, Is the Holy Spirit and your conscience the same thing?

    - 1 Corinthians 4:4

    - Romans 2:14–15

    - 1 Corinthians 2:10–13

Prayer Requests

♥ **Make It Personal: Journal Notes** ♥

CHAPTER 7

Failure: Is It a Roadblock or Pathway to Freedom?

> For we all stumble in many ways.
> —James 3:2a (NAS)

When I have set out to accomplish a task and have not achieved the desired results I feel like a failure. This will often make me feel as if somehow I am insufficient. At times in your life you have felt like a failure. Make a list of some things at which you feel you have failed. Set this list aside to use later in this lesson.

When you think of failure, your focus is often on yourself, your dreams, and your accomplishments. But consider what failure is from God's point of view. A careful study of the Bible shows that most Bible characters failed at times in their lives. By studying the lives of these people, you can learn what God wants you to know about failure.

Consider Failure in the Lives of Theses Biblical People

Hannah

Read Hannah's story in 1 Samuel 1:1–23. Then answer the following questions.

1. What happened in Hannah's life that made her feel like she was a failure (1 Samuel 1:6)?

2. When she felt like her life was a failure, what action did she choose (1 Samuel 1:10)?

3. As a result of Hannah praying, what did God do (1 Samuel 1:19–20)?

4. How long had Hannah felt like a failure before God changed the circumstances of her life (1 Samuel 1:7)?

Discuss the following questions. What emotions do you think Hannah felt during this time of her life? Was there a time in your life when you experienced similar emotions?

When we read 1 Samuel 1:1–23, we can actually feel Hannah's pain. Hannah did not sin in her desire to have children, yet her circumstances left her unhappy. The culture she lived in made her feel like she was a failure for not having children.

Two things Hannah can teach you:
- Godly people with right motives will experience failure. Hannah felt like a failure because she had not given Elkanah any children.
- There is a time to get off your knees and take action. For Hannah, that time was when God spoke to her through the priest.

5. What change do you see in Hannah that showed she trusted God?

Ask Yourself

When God gives you a promise, do you let it show as confidence and joy in your face? Does your behavior change? When Hannah trusted God, her countenance changed; her face was no longer sad. Her behavior showed she had faith in God's promise to her.

Peter

Read Matthew 14:23–33, and answer the following questions.

6. What is Peter's request?

7. As a result of looking at the wind, what happed to Peter?

8. How did Jesus respond?

Peter is often criticized for taking his eyes off Jesus rather than being praised for having the courage to step out and try to do the impossible. When Peter took his eyes off Jesus, Jesus did not criticize Peter but reached out in love to take his hand to help him back up.

9. What is the result of Peter's failure?

Two thing you can learn from Peter:
- Matthew 14:33 says all those who were in the boat worshipped Jesus. If your failure causes God to be worshipped, is it a failure or a success? You need to learn to see things from God's perspective. The things you view as failures, God uses as tools to accomplish His purpose in your life and in the lives of other people.
- We learn that in the midst of problems is not a time to interpret God's will. As Peter was sinking, he did not ask Jesus, "Is it Your will for me to walk on water?" Peter simply cried out for help. It was a time to cry out to God and experience His unconditional love.

10. Describe what has happened in Luke 22:54–62.

11. If you had been Peter, how would you have felt when Jesus turned and looked at you? Can you share a time in your life you actually felt that way?

12. After Jesus turned and looked at Peter, what was Peter's response?

Peter responded with a heart of repentance. This experience prepared Peter for what Jesus was going to ask him to do. After Jesus's resurrection, Jesus asks Peter to "tend my lambs." In Jesus's absence, Jesus asked Peter to become a pastor and teacher to other believers.

Write next to these verses what Peter learned from his failure.
- Proverbs 29:25

- Acts 5:29

- Romans 8:1

When you fear other people more than God, you lose your freedom in Christ. It keeps you from experiencing the abundant life God has for you.

Ask Yourself

Are there times in your life when you made a poor decision? Can you see how God used that experience to strengthen you or prepare you for His future plans for you?

Like Peter, we all fail. When you are feeling like a failure is the time to remember the promises of God. This is one of God's promises that I often remind myself of: "The steps of a man are established by the Lord, and he delights in his way. When he falls, he shall not be hurled headlong, because the Lord is the one who holds his hand" (Psalm 37:23–24 NAS).

Make a list of the promises God has given to you.

Job

Job must have felt like a failure because he lost so much. When Job's friends came to visit, they told him all these things happened to him because he sinned.

13. Read Job 1:12–19 and 2:7. What happened to Job? What did Job lose?

Job lost everything—his possessions, his children, and his health. The only thing he did not lose was his wife.
Three of Job's friends came to visit him. Next to their names, write what each friend said to Job.
- Eliphaz (Job 4:8)

- Bildad (Job 8:4–6)

- Zophar (Job 11:13–16)

What you can learn from Job:
- The counsel of others is never a wise substitute for the counsel of God (Job 38:1–2).

- It is never right to blame God (Job 1:22).
- The best comfort you can give to a friend is just to be with him or her (Job 2:11–13).

Make It Personal

Job never knew why he suffered and failed. It was during this time that Job encountered God. Have the times you suffered and failed brought you closer to God?

Joseph

If you do not know the story of Joseph, you can read it in Genesis 37–50. He was treated unfairly again and again. Yet, in Genesis 50:20, Joseph makes an amazing conclusion about these events. Joseph says to his brothers, "You meant it for harm, but God meant it for good." Joseph was able to view his life from God's perspective. Romans 8:28 tells us all thing work together for those who love the Lord. This does not mean all things in our life are good. It does mean God will use all the events in your life to bring about His purpose. Joseph understood this to be true in his life.

Each of the following verses teaches you a biblical truth you need to remember when you go through hard times. Match the verse with the statement that goes with the reference.

a. Hebrews 4:16 ___We are God's workmanship.
b. Psalm 37:34 ___We receive the love, grace, and mercy in our time of need.
c. Proverbs 16:1–4 ___God has a plan for our lives, and it may be different from ours.
d. Philippians 1:6 ___God has begun a good work in you and will finish it.

e. Ephesians 2:10 ___For those who love the Lord, all things work together for good.
f. Romans 8:28 ___We learn to wait on God.

Points to Ponder

You must learn to look at the events in your life from God's eternal perspective, not our shortsighted worldly view. Second Corinthians 4:17 tells you that the suffering you are experiencing is light and momentary. At the moment, you feel like you have failed. It is hard to understand that God is accomplishing something with an eternal value. You need to change the way you think. Renew your mind to accept your failures as a blessing from God.

Make It Personal

Go back to the list of things at which you feel you have failed. As you reconsider this list, do you have a new perspective? Can you see where these experiences helped you to grow spiritually?

Dig Deeper

Make a list of as many biblical characters as you can. Next to each name write down the things in their lives that made them feel like they failed. Put an asterisk by each name the world would view as a failure. Put a cross by each name where God received glory, honor, or praise. Consider how many times the world would view an experience as a failure, yet it brought glory to God. Learning to see things from God's point of view will change you. This will allow you to experience the freedom you are searching for.

Prayer Requests

♥ **Make It Personal: Journal Notes** ♥

Leader's Guide

This study guide was designed to use in a small-group or individual study. Included here are additional information and suggestions to aid in having a group discussion. In each chapter, there are places that say, "Make It Personal." I recommend you use the page at the end of each chapter to maintain a personal journal as you go through this study. Journaling increases your focus, gives you a deeper level of learning, and boosts memory.

Chapter 1: Freedom in Christ

1. Jesus asked for a drink for the purpose of engaging this woman in conversation. Both Jesus and the woman knew that drinking out of the same cup as a Samaritan would have made him ceremonially unclean, requiring the process of purification, which would cause Him to wait seven days before He could worship at the temple. Jesus's example shows that sometimes you need to do the unexpected to get an opportunity to share the message of salvation.
2. The woman told Jesus she did not have a husband. She was not acknowledging the complete truth. She had been married five times and was currently living with a man. This is often how we deal with our sin. We tell partial truths and think it is all right. We fail to tell people the complete truth about what we are doing.
3. Jesus told the woman things no stranger would know. Jesus told her she was married five times and was currently

living with a man. Notice how Jesus responded honestly to the women yet did not express any condemnation. The Samaritan woman would have had access to the Old Testament and may have known passages like Psalm 44:21 or Psalm 37. These passages tell about God knowing the secret things of the heart. Thus, she concluded that Jesus was a prophet.

4. The question she asks is: Where should men worship? Worship has been an issue people have argued over both in Jesus's day and today. Jesus uses the issue of worship to bring people closer to God.

5. This question had great importance because the Jews worshipped at one temple (in Jerusalem) and the Samaritans at another (on Mount Gerizim). The Jews believed the one true God could only be worshipped in one place. The Jews believed people who worshipped anywhere else did not worship the one true God. Jesus turned the conversation from where to worship to who you worship. In John 4:24 (NAS) Jesus states, "God is spirit; those who worship Him must worship in spirit and truth."

    Special Note: As the leader of the group, this is your opportunity to discuss who you worship.

    "Christ died for our sins according to the scriptures, and that He was buried, and that He was raised on the third day according to the scriptures" (1 Corinthians 15:3b–4 NAS). Leaders, do you know if each member of your group has accepted Jesus as their Savior?

6. The Samaritan woman believed Jesus was the promised Messiah. Here it is indicated she knew scripture. The prophet Daniel had spoken of a Messiah who will make an end to sin and bring in eternal righteousness (Daniel 9:24).

7. The woman's response was to go and tell others. Acts 1:8 tells us we must be a witness.

8. Jesus wanted the disciples to understand that they would be the ones to go into the entire world to share the good news that Jesus is the Messiah. Jesus had come to save the people from their sin, not from a corrupt government system, which is what the Jewish people were hoping for.

Make It Personal

Write in the journal notes the names of people you could share Christ with. Next to each name write what excuse you have given for not sharing the gospel with them.

Dig Deeper

Share with each other what you think it means to know Jesus. Write in your journal what it means for you to know Jesus. Is Jesus the Lord or ruler of your life? If you are to make Jesus the Lord of your life, what changes might you consider making in your life?

Chapter 2: Abiding in Christ

Ways to Abide in My Word

Match the following verses with the way it tells us we can abide.
f, a, g, h, b, e, c, d

Be Creative

Try to have a verse to back up each suggestion. Take time to write down all the ideas the group suggests. Here are a few suggestions.
Your attitude—Philippians 4:5
Singing praise—Acts 16:25
Praying—1 Thessalonians 5:17a
Giving thanks—1 Thessalonians 5:18

A True Disciple

1. A true disciple will be like his or her teacher. We are in the process of becoming like Jesus. Like an athlete, we are to be focused on our goal of becoming like Jesus. This is a good time to discuss what things are distracting us from accomplishing our goals.

Personal Application

- This is a great opportunity to encourage each other. Make this a positive time.
- Have a discussion, and write in your journal (journaling may be done at home).

You Will Know the Truth

2. Here Jesus uses some very strong words. You cannot hear or understand because you are not of God; you are of your father, the devil. Now is the time for salvation. As the leader of a small group, talk about what it means for God to be your heavenly Father.
3. Finding the way is through a narrow gate, and few find it.

The Truth Sets You Free

4. We are no longer in bondage to sin, therefore, sin has no power over us.
5. What do these verses say about bondage?
- Romans 6:6–7: Sin may be in this world, but sin no longer has any power to control us. Through the power of Christ, we are free from the bondage of sin.
- Romans 6:14: Sin is not our master, but the grace of God has given us power over sin.

Dig Deeper

6. What do these verses tell you about abiding in Christ?
- 1 John 3:24

    We know we are abiding in Christ when we keep His commandments.
- 1 John 3:6

    When we abide in Christ, we do not sin. This means we do not choose a lifestyle of sin.
- 1 John 2:27

    When we abide in Christ, we have the Holy Spirit teaching us to know what the truth is and what is a lie.
- 1 John 4:13

    We have been given His spirit. We abide in Him, and He abides in us.

Chapter 3: Know Who You Are

When you close your eyes and think about yourself, who is the person you see. Write in the journal notes what you see.

The Way You Think Is How You Act

1. All the men agreed the land was fertile and a great place to live. They called it a land flowing with milk and honey. The men reported the inhabitants of the land were very powerful, and the cities were large and fortified.
2. Caleb said that they should go in and take the land God gave them. He believed God wanted to bless them. No matter how hopeless the circumstances looked, he was willing to trust God.
3. The other men spread a bad report among the Israelites. They compared the people to giants and themselves to grasshoppers. In other words, they were saying they felt like helpless creatures compared to the people of the land.

4. They were weeping, crying, blaming their leader, and not accepting any responsibility for themselves. The people felt it would be better to choose another leader and to go back to Egypt.
5. God would give them victory over their enemies and give them the land.

See Yourself through God's Eyes

- Psalms 139:14–16: I am fearfully and wonderfully made.
- Genesis 1:26–27: I am made in the image and likeness of God.
- John 15:9: Jesus loves me.
- Hebrews 12:6–7: I am a child of God's.
- 2 Corinthians 12:9: The power of Christ dwells in me.
- Matthew 6:26: I am worth more than the birds of the field who God takes care of.
- John 17:22–23: I am one with God.
- Philippians 4:13: With God I can do all things.

The Enemy of Sin and Guilt

6. They felt fear, guilt, and shame for the first time. Guilt and shame are different from each other. Guilt says to us, "I did something wrong." Shame says to us, "I am a mistake." Adam and Eve had never experienced any of these emotions, and God needed to help them learn how to manage their emotions. When you sin, you should feel guilt, confess your sin (1 John 1:9), and accept God's forgiveness.

Personal Application

As a group, you can discuss these questions. As individuals, take time to write in your journal.

The Enemy of Comparison

7. When you compare yourself with others, it shows you are without spiritual understanding. Leaders, take the time to read Ephesians 4:18 and 2 Corinthians 3:14.

The Enemy of Listening to Other People

8. There will always be someone who will curse you, put you down, or gossip about you. People will say many things; do not take all things personally. It is what God says about you that matters.
9. Talk about God having a special plan for everyone and how these plans are for our good.

Your Thoughts Can Be the Enemy

10. Proverbs 23:7 tells us a person will act in accordance to what he or she thinks. What you tell yourself and what you think about is what you become.
11. Every thought you have should be surrendered to Christ and His way of thinking.

Chapter 4: I Have Been Forgiven

Accepting God's Forgiveness

Human love is very often given conditionally. Conditional love says, "You must agree with me," or, "Act in a manner I approve of to receive my love."

1. Leviticus 20:10 and Deuteronomy 22:22 state the adulterer and the adulteress should be put to death.
2. Jesus stooped down and wrote in the ground.

3. The one without sin is to throw the first stone.
4. Jesus asked her, "Where are those who have accused you?"
5. Perhaps Jesus wrote the names of her accusers and/or the sins that they had committed.

What about My Sinful Past?

6. Old things are in the past; we must forget what lies behind us. The old is gone. God has given you a fresh start. Forget the past, and move forward into the new life in Christ.

An Example of a Changed Life

7. He was dragging Christian men and woman off to prison in an attempt to destroy the church.
8. Saul was on the road to Damascus when he was blinded by a bright light from heaven and heard Jesus's voice. Jesus tells him to go into the city and wait for instructions. In the city, Ananias finds Saul. Ananias lays hands on Saul and restores his sight. Saul, filled with the Holy Spirit, was baptized.

Spiritual Growth

Use this time to share how God is working in each of their lives and what changes have occurred.

But I Do Not Feel Forgiven

When you do not forgive yourself, you make yourself more important than God. This is a form of idolatry.

9. Paul states what a miserable man he was when he let sin dominate his life.

10. The apostle Paul points us to the only place where freedom can be found—in Jesus Christ.
11. When we are in Christ God does not condemn us, and He gives us power over sin.

Your Position in Christ

- Galatians 2:20: It is no longer I but (*Christ who*) lives in me.
- Ephesians 1:5: I am adopted into (*the family of God*).
- 2 Corinthians: I am (*righteous*).
- Romans 5:1: I am (*justified*) or (*declared righteous*) by God.
- Ephesians 1:1: I am a (*saint*).
- Ephesians 1:4: I am (*holy and blameless*).
- Ephesians 1:3: I have (*every spiritual blessing*).
- Ephesians 2:6: I am seated with (*Him in heavenly places*).

12. What do the following verses tell you the Holy Spirit will do for you?
    John 14:26: The Holy Spirit is our *helper,* and He will *teach you all things.*
    John 16:13: When the Spirit comes, He will *guide us into the truth.*
    1 Corinthians 2:10–16: The Spirit shows us the *deep truths of God.* The Spirit is from *God.* The things of the Spirit are *foolishness* to the natural man. The Spirit gives us the *mind* of Christ.
    1 Corinthians 12:13–14: We are all baptized into one *Spirit,* and we all receive the *Spirit.*

Dig Deeper

13. What do these verses teach us about God's forgiveness?
    1 John 2:12: Sins are forgiven because of Jesus.

Ephesians 1:17: By the grace of God the price was paid for the forgiveness of our sins.

Psalm 103:12: Our sins are removed from us as far as the east is from the west, which is something that cannot be measured.

Colossians 1:13: With God's forgiveness, we have been moved into His kingdom.

Psalm 32:5: When I confessed my sins to God and stopped trying to hide from Him, He forgave me, and all my guilt is gone.

Hebrews 10:17: God does not remember our sins.

Chapter 5: Managing Emotions God's Way

Ask each person to write down how they feel. Have a few people share how they feel.

Why Did God Give You Emotions?

1. What are the emotions God has expressed in the following verses?
   - Numbers 32:13   anger
   - Psalm 37:13   joy
   - Judges 2:18   compassion
   - Psalm 78:40   grief
   - John 3:16   love
   - Psalm 5:5   hatred
   - Exodus 20:5   jealousy

2. God expresses love; He loved us first, so we would return His love.
3. God sent His Son, Jesus, to give His life in our place. When we see fellow believers in need, we should do what we can to help them.

4. Philippians 4:7: The peace of God will be in your heart.
   1 Thessalonians 5:16: You will have the ability to rejoice in all things.

Sin Affected Your Emotions

5. Adam and Eve saw their nakedness and experienced sexual lust, shame, and guilt. And then they feared God. Sexual lust means their desire was to please themselves more than the other person.

The Sin Nature

6. The power of our sin nature has been taken away by the crucifixion of Christ.
7. We are told to lay aside the old nature. Let our thoughts and attitudes be renewed. We are to be transformed into a new person who is Christ-like.

Damaged Emotions

8. A renewal of the mind means the removal of our old way of thinking and replacing it with God's way of thinking.
9. God promises to heal the brokenhearted and help those who are afflicted with grief and trouble to give them peace.

God's Intentions for Your Emotions

10. Write next to each verse what the Bible tells you the abundant life will look like.
    Galatians 5:22–23: In our lives we should be experiencing love, joy, peace, patience, kindness, goodness and gentleness.

Colossians 3:2–3: We find our thoughts focused on Christ and not on ourselves.

1 Corinthians 2:9: God has prepared for us more than we can imagine.

Ephesians 3:20: God will do for us more than we can ask or think of.

11. We experience the abundant life when we let Christ live through us. Our focus is not on ourselves but on God.

Emotions Are Intended to Motivate You to Take Action

12. What emotion is felt, who felt it, and what action was taken as a result of that emotion?
    - John 3:16: God's love for us caused Him to send His son to die for our sins.
    - 1 Samuel 1:10: Hannah was deeply distressed, which caused her to pray. God answered her prayer, and she gave birth to the great prophet Samuel.
    - 11 Samuel 18:8–11: Anger and Jealousy caused King Saul to throw a spear at David as he played the harp.

Dig Deeper

13. In 1 Kings 11:9–11, God is angry at Solomon for worshipping other gods. The nation of Israel would be taken from him; it would not be passed to one of his sons.
14. Matthew 20:34: Jesus showed compassion to a blind man; touching his eyes, Jesus restored his sight.
15. Looking around at people who are expressing their emotions, we see acts of violence and selfishness far more than acts of kindness. In other words, we see the actions of the sinful nature not the fruit of the spirit (Galatians 5:19).

It is not the emotion that is sinful but the action that the person has chosen.
16. The devil is hunting his prey, seeking someone to destroy.
17. We are to submit to God.

Chapter 6: Your Conscience: Can You Trust It?

1. Write next to each verse what it tells you about your conscience.
    Acts 23:1: Paul stated that before God, he had a good conscience.
    Acts 24:16: We should maintain a blameless conscience before people and God.
    1 Peter 3:16: Keep a good conscience so that when someone speaks against you, it is invalid.
    Hebrews 13:18: We have a good conscience; pray we continue to do good.
2. These verses describe a *good* or *blameless* conscience.
3. Titus 1:15 describes a *defiled or corrupted* conscience. Hebrews 9:14 tells us that the *blood of Christ* will *cleanse* our consciences.
4. In 1 Corinthians 8:7, a weak conscience is described.
5. A spiritually mature believer would choose not participate in an activity that might cause another believer, who has a weak conscience, to struggle with the person's spiritual walk.

Paul Teaches Timothy

6. 1 Timothy 1:5: When we give instructions, we should have a heart that is right with God and a clear conscience.
    1 Timothy 1:18–19: Fight the good fight keeping a clear conscience.

1 Timothy 3:8–9: Deacons in the church must have a clear conscience.

1 Timothy 4:1–2: People with a seared conscience will fall away from the faith.

2 Timothy 1:3: I am thankful to serve God with a clear conscience.

7. Your conscience can become damaged, and it cannot then guide you in a godly manner.
8. Your conscience can become defiled or seared. "Seared" is a term used for something burned that is often not repairable. When you burn a shirt with a hot iron, the seared marks from the iron are almost always impossible to remove. This is the damage you do to your conscience.
9. Good conscience: Keeping the faith; holding to the truth taught by Jesus.

   Clear conscience: Fight the good fight means to put away the old and be renewed through Christ.

   Seared or branded conscience: A conscience that is damaged by sinning against God.
10. People often think that if their consciences do not bother them, they must be right with God. You are not to rely on your conscience but the truth that is written in God's Word.

    Match the Following

    c, d, b, e, f, a

David Listens to His Conscience

11. To take the life of King Saul.
12. He cut off the corner of Saul's robe.
13. David's conscience spoke to him. He could not harm the Lord's anointed.
14. David refused to let anyone harm King Saul.
15. It is an example of how God can use a good conscience.

Dig Deeper

16. Are the Holy Spirit and your conscience the same things?
    - 1 Corinthians 4:4: My conscience might be innocent but that does not make me innocent before God.
    - Romans 2:14–15: Their consciences bear witness, accusing or defending them.
    - 1 Corinthians 2:10–13: God reveals things to us through the Spirit.

After reading these verses, it is clear that the Holy Spirit and your conscience are not the same. God speaks directly to you through His Spirit. God can use a renewed conscience to help guide you, but the conscience can also deceive you. The conscience is renewed just as your mind is renewed by spending time in God's Word.

Chapter 7: Failure: Is It a Roadblock or a Pathway to Freedom

Hannah

1. Hannah had no children, and Peninnah, Elkanah's other wife, would provoke her.
2. Hannah went to God to cry and to pour out her heart in prayer.
3. God spoke through the priest to tell her that her prayer had been answered. After returning home, she conceived a son.
4. We do not know the exact amount of time, but it was years because Peninnah had sons and daughters.
   Discuss the following question: In the culture in which Hannah lived, a woman's value was based on her ability to give her husband children. Hannah had no children, and Peninnah not only had several children but provoked Hannah. Hannah would have felt like a miserable, worthless

failure. This is seen in 1 Samuel 1:8 where Elkanah comments on her crying, her sad heart, and her not eating.
5. Hannah got up and went back to the feast with her face no longer sad, and she ate.

Peter

6. Peter asked to come to the Lord on the water.
7. Peter saw the wind, became frightened, and began to sink into the water.
8. Immediately, Jesus stretches out His hand to help Peter.
9. All of those in the boat worshipped Jesus, saying that He was indeed God's Son.
10. Jesus had been arrested. Peter had gone into the courtyard by the fire, where, after he was accused three times of being a follower of Jesus, he denied knowing Him.
11. Peter felt the guilt of sin and embarrassment of doing exactly what he said he would never do. As for me, I am like Peter, I am full of pride. I say I would never lie, yet when questioned by someone to avoid personal embarrassment, I find myself telling a lie.
12. Peter ran out of the court and wept bitterly. Then he repented of his sin.

Write next to these verses what Peter learned from his failure:

Proverbs 29:25: Human fear keeps us in bondage. It caused Peter to deny knowing Jesus.

Acts 5:29: Peter learned to obey God rather than a human.

Romans 8:1: Peter learned that even though he denied Jesus, he was not condemned. God used Peter's failure to prepare him for the future God had for him. Jesus later asked Peter to take care of those who chose to follow Him.

Job

13. Satan was allowed to test Job's faith in God. Job lost all he owned as well as his children. After that, Job lost his health. Write what each friend said.

    Eliphaz (Job 4:8): Those who do evil will get evil returned back to themselves.

    Bildad (Job 8:4–6): Your children must have sinned against God for He took them. If you would seek God and be pure and rightous, these things would not happen to you.

    Zophar (Job 11:13–16): You have let sin into your house, and you must stop sinning. You need to devote yourself totally to God.

    Match the verse with the statement that goes with the reference.

    b, f, c, d, a, e